T0146699

SCOPPETRY

Anthony C Murphy

authorHOUSE®

AuthorHouse™
1663 Liberty Drive
Bloomington, IN 47403
www.authorhouse.com
Phone: 1 (800) 839-8640

Published by AuthorHouse   04/18/2017

ISBN: 978-1-5246-8864-6 (sc)
ISBN: 978-1-5246-8863-9 (e)

Library of Congress Control Number: 2017904194

Print information available on the last page.

This book is printed on acid-free paper.

Acknowledgements

Fall Ferment appeared in Blue Door Quarterly Volume 2.1
The Leatherman appeared in Westchester Review 2017

For Valerie

A LIGHTBULB IN HULL'S CHANCE

I asked Larkin
How many parents does it take to screw
Up a childhood
All of them
And it's fuck up
When you're from Coventry
He said quietly
Licking his pencil
As a toad tongues a fly

WHY VISIT RUINS

She sleeps
Fretfully
Quivering next to me
As I hold her small foot in my old fist
In a king-sized sick bed in Mexico

We listen
To the hidden lizard
In the thatch above us
Clucking a yah boo response to
Wet grackles outside looking for a morsel

It rains
All morning
And the fans give in
As the grid temps out
We sweat into ourselves as animals

And I made myself say
All will be well after breakfast
But the kid's insides flip out
And I wash her hair free of egg white and banana
We play igames instead of swimming in the sea
We all drink pedialyte instead of beer

NORTHERN GENII

A thumbnail moon snaggles up for the night
Caught comfy in the baggy black pullover of the sky

Warm animal life in this Northern town is dumb now
And all insects dry
Even the moths are dust

A genie slicks through the crepuscular streets
A muscular brain no one follows
No one knows as no one hears
Ears usually attuned to the tinkle of coins on the pavement
Eyes to their corners, straining
Ready to come out fighting
There is no time to think
There is no room to breathe
To earn only and exist
No ideas here
Yet
There is a name on the tip of all tongues
Genius
What was it?
Hold that thought
He is lexical access incarnate
The answer personified
And yet the city lets him slide
Right on

He glides by like a football on a wet Sunday morning
During your pub team's eleven-a-side struggle
To get going
Crapulous Athletic Nil
Hungover Academicals Nil

And would any one for once pick him to play?
- Who needs to score?
It's all about not losing here
Especially against them there

The genius sidles off down south
Through rainbow ridden puddles
Splashing in streets of toxic gold

OUR LIFE IS LIQUID

We drink up familiar roads in the rain
Roads lined with half abandoned mills
And while it is not yet light
These semi shattered brick monsters loom over us
As they always have

The roads look slick with 6 a.m drizzle
So we head for the ginnell
To the grass of the canal bank
And uncork a bottle
As we celebrate the end of another shift

We watch the purple light start
On any movement in the water
And even though I listen to Joe
Yawn with the effort of advice
My last thought is that loss
Has no need for sleep

A blackbird sings
He is a loud one
Who else to waken everything
Proud and first and loudest
He is joined later by others of dull colours
Some that can't sing
Like the gulls who try without a syrinx

And my first thought is of her

How we let us slip
Because we are fluid and hard to hold on to
Like a single teardrop

It's too early now to have quality sleep
There are songs to be sung anyhow
Before dawn
We are beneath a symphony again

And she always said
I hate music

JIMMY'S CLIFF

The sea is no less inviting today
Seen here from this blue and terrible height
It is mobile with white flicks or silver
In flight, flecks of never, undetermined

To wish for the depths seems ridiculous
But dizziness affects more than the feet
A fool's dancing head on a beach full of
Clouds out of reach is forever ending

THE RAG CANAL

Well in the suffocating month of August
As even the few rain spurts failed
We took to swimming in our own back yard neck of the
    woods
There the canal was
And a more enticing prospect than the river Roche
Which was closer
And more approachable
For the likes of rats
And shopping carts
And hooligans
Plus, there is no real flow to a canal
The stagnant nature of it
Although a breeding ground for god knows what
Meant that we could sedately
Tread
Water
We were dogs and hippos
None of this whooping and bombing and belly flopping
Kids off a pier
No white horses, no foam, no splash, here

Eye level with a towpath of history
Looking at the smashed windows of the big old mills
All of this unused and no danger
The grasses untouched for decades
Waving their beards
Perch could be nibbling

Us bobbing like silly buoys
Taut muscles menaced by student pike
Until dark
Inbetween the stillness

SHE'S NOT A RIVER YET

He asks me
My brother
What is it like?
It's like a trickle that becomes a sea
This new one
She is not even a rivulet
Although she babbles at moments
I say
Do you remember that brook trout you caught
Under the discarded metal sheet from the factory
It struggled
One short muscle
It was like that
All different colours though

THE LEATHERMAN

On the wind
Wet cowhide
Old tokes and sweat
Before we heard that rattle breath
Once every moon
Then his creak into our village

"Leave be! He's doing his thing", she would say
Motherwise and caring
"The soft lad!"

We laughed anyway and threw rotten crops
That bounced off that stiff old steer suit
He would only catch the bread or tobacco
Our parents could heft

One fall
Jack's nose nearly caught the waft of his cane
We kept our heads after that
Studied his circus instead
Slow and loopy like the days were then

We knew he slept as a bear
In caves cold with fire
Or kept to the glades
In the off pace of summer
And that he had no tongue
Yet could talk to the world that he walked

After the last war
When only some came running back
He was a giant in our brains
We wondered at his freedom

Then one month the vagabond didn't appear
Not the smell nor the creak nor the need
And that was all for his adventure
But we were out of our gate
With provisions
At any hint
Any whiff of smoke and leather

MUSIC AND LAUGHTER

Our kitchen was filled with music and laughter when I was
    a child
The tinkling music of dishes miswashed
Broken bottles
The sinking songs of dreams lost in the swirl
Down the plughole
And the hard braying laughter
At all of it
Of how dare you dream
We jumped to its tune
As we spun on our heels
Heads full of toothless grins
And fantasies of avoidance

NOON TOOT

There's a picture stuck on the flue, some glam motor oil
   promo
The nubile girl is lubed and pneumatic
The picture covers a hole in the old chimney of
This once manufactory
That's now used as a weld supply shop
Though lads are still coated in grease caked overalls
The workers in and out of
These once red brick walls
Trade nuts and bolts instead of molten metal

They're unaware of the revolution that went on
Them, as us, just apprentices earning beer and fag money
They all existing in the moments

The girl in the picture starts to twitch
There is a movement beneath her left tit
The poster flicks from the wall a bit
Two apprentices notice

The fuck was that?
To Dave, asks Pete
T'were probably just
The wind, says Dave, farting in reply

The girl's nipple extends then
The thought of someone behind her poking with a pen, is
That what could be happening

Then, wonders Pete, as he walks to the flue
Talking to the 'someone' trapped in
The chimney
They take the picture off
The wall says farewell Miss January

There is the yellow bill of a desperate bird
Tap tap tapping now at fresher air
Trapped like a feathered star

There is a gasp from all three
There are three gasps
Try to pull the thing
Through, it's what to do
Through
The hole
'Tis the beak beak
That doesn't work
'Tis the head too big, warbles Pete
They try to make the hole bigger
The bird keeps poking in
To chip away would kill it

The bird's beak starts to gape

They manage to get some water to the throat
That dust you know
They stand undecided

Then the whistle for dinner blows

Tissue gets stuffed into the hole
Tissue with which they push back the starling

They stick Miss February back over
The discomfort and then
To the chippy they tootle off
Towards a mushy pea fritter

Tear into your dinner like lads let loose for their pint of
    bitter
Tear another day off the calendar lads!

FALL FERMENT

Your cold voice calls at four in the morning
Through the gap I had left
For night's stale breath
Before sun or gull's elemental yawns
You drunkenly whisper of death

And take me with you this rotten harvest
Bury us deep, slow the blood in our chests
We sleep until spring leans its leaves to the wind
Green in our dreams free of care

BEDDYSEY

I was trying to get a ride home
One time
I stood there and watched
The mirrored confusion on the faces
Of some of the braking drivers
As they then drove on
Is he drunk?
The thought process goes
Am I?
We all have the same look
In our eyes
At that nighttime

It was 1987
And there're no taxis
In my town
And anyway I am drunkenly out of money
Like a kid
And there are no buses
So I thumb and walk
And shrug my shoulders to
Suggest it's your turn to
Kelvin and Jason
As they step next to me
Coming out of the bushes at the side of the road

Kelvin is a psychobilly
With a quiff that punctures clouds
He carries a knife in his beetle crushers

And an attitude to boot
Anyone
Even friends on a nine mile walk home

Jason is my brother
Literally
He is into Miami Vice and wears day glo socks
But that was in the past
And he is my brother

We have listened to music together
And understood
We stood under
The beautiful thunder of
Some old band or other
Or was it only The Housemartin's drummer

We got spat on by misplaced punks
This is not why we're here

It was a bad gig
By all accounts
But we loved it

We had gone and gotten ourselves there
In amongst it
The Manchester rabble
The death of the punk
The birth of the indie
At the age of 16
It seems old but we had been caught up on Queen
And Genesis

And anything white inbetween
Days of no cure
Or bunnymen
The first band we saw were The Proclaimers

And now we are walking home

Kelvin walks into a lamppost
Sparks himself out on the path
We pick him up and hold him
Between us
Me and Jason talk as Kelvin breathes

We should get going
What was your favourite bit
Come on
Sing it
Happy Hour
You are such a capitalist
Yes that one
Kelvin can walk
When is the next bus
In two hours
We'll be home by then
We might be
Let's walk
We have to
It'll be good
Let's just walk
Wake up
It's happy hour again

Kelvin rouses himself at the last
Refrain

Kelvin roused himself
Refrain!

The three of us are mobile again

We wander through Prestwich and by Heaton Park
Why not sleep there
We wonder
And remember the pope in '82
And the trouble we all went through then
The thievery
The day glo bracelets that leaked onto infant skin
That burned
And we remember the cold clear night
And none of us with blankets
Just our burgeoning conversations about girls and the world
In that order

I am tired
I say
So J
And Kelvin
Squash me in as we keep our legs moving
And wander on to Rochdale

Remembering the one-eyed man
Who gave us a dance in Harpurhey
Outside of Bernard Manning's place
He's hilarious

Until he zips up his pants
And gets carted away
There's nothing to see anymore

In Middleton we hear the sigh
Of a thousand parting legs
Too many pubs
Too many pickled eggs
So many farts

All that is left to digest
Is Heywood
It might take a while
We can walk through Ashworth Valley
And remember
Fat Tom's head
Spank worthy like a raw chicken
Mud ovens with black potatoes
Flour twists
A clean brook with no chance of trout
White supremacists in boy scout uniforms
At every turn
Youth and beauty and everything to learn
And rebellion
And on
To Rochdale and
Home

Just another bed
To escape from

ENTWINED

I know you like the back of my hand
I know I don't like yours

We tickle each other
Do we not
From miles apart
On the phone

He gasps his laughter
Into the night but

The laughs
The slacks
The suit
The shoes
The books
The bookies
The fags
The brandy
The, Christ!
The dog
The gasps

When the final call comes
Out of nowhere
Over there
He has left without all of the above

HAVE THE CHILD ASSEMBLE
THE PUZZLE

She prays to pink and occasionally purple
She worships worms
There are only three letters in her alphabet
And two of them are the same
Her geography is a straight river
And a blueberry bush that traps catbirds
Under a flushing dogwood tree
Her clothes are historical
And her laugh is vintage
She scatters fear with ignorance
And only cries five times a day
Have the child assemble the puzzle
Give yourself time off with no pay

MY FIRES

When they knocked on the door
And handed him
His scarecrow frame flopped over the threshold
In and out of consciousness
"Keep him hydrated"
The police woman said
"He hasn't done anything illegal but he made us chase him
    and I slipped in dogshit so I'm not happy."
I couldn't help but grin at that as I put the wood in the hole.
14 and his friends had treated him like a guinea pig with E's
    instead of sugar cubes.
It reminded me of that asthma attack he had when I had
    to carry him up the hill away from cat hair. He's over six
    foot now but skinny.
Whatever shall we do with you? Have we failed? Or are you
    just mad?
I didn't grow up until…
And I still do crazy things
As did granddad
Maybe it's genetic
Maybe there is something better to take
Some better pill
Because this bitterness
This dry lack of joy
Has extinguished me

When you were born
Big and bloody

You turned your mother inside out
She lost most of herself on the red table
And stayed there for a week
I had you for months as mine
We stitched together some time
As the wounds healed
You were fat and happy
We were all young
We lost and won then
Your mother lost most

Whenever I have to deal with my own physical trauma
The concussions or incarcerations
Of which there have been many
I do not fear
I feel at home
My fires are those when I watch hot others burn so close to me

OUR LIFE IS LIQUID X

We were on holiday and we needed it. We needed some kind of reconnection, even though we had just gotten back together. We needed to take ourselves out of our landlocked lives, to sea, to see.

Bodrum is on the west coast of Turkey, making it a tourist destination for a mix of Europeans who play it safe in the Mediterranean. The ones who don't want to stray too far East, or South. In our hotel everybody seemed to be from Yorkshire, old Yorkshire. Turns out that Doncaster, the remodeled Robin Hood Airport, had direct flights to Bodrum, cheap and available.

We had flown in from London Gatwick but I guess the passengers on our flight had booked into other hotels, so here we were with a cocktail of British Northerners. It's not exactly an exclusive club, and one you might want to escape from, but when abroad… Let's just say I've been a card-carrying member my whole life, so I was a cack caked pig, but she, Olivia, being from the south, she wasn't happy. I had reverted to type.

After another night of charred steak and raki and salad and raki and a late stumble home through the pomegranate grove and passing out by the pool, Olivia decided to expand our horizons. We were going on some package tour.

We boarded a bus outside of the slipper baths. Our guide was a twenty-odd year old with good English, thick glasses and a pencil moustache. His name was Taki, and he would be our guide, he said, welcome to Bodrum.

The bus made several stops and was soon full of the chatter of Italia and Germania and Great Britannia.

I had a hat that I pulled down over my nose as Olivia got to know our bus neighbours, using some kind of Esperanto body language. I could feel her affirmative head bobbing next to me as I nodded off. Is that what I want to say? Beneath the murmur murmur, I could see her "Right! Right! Yes! I get it!" positivity, and her willingness to listen. I could see it with my eyes closed. I could feel her non-genuine smile. I could hear it stretch across her lips.

The beach wasn't great where we were staying so I was glad to investigate a little, but this bus had caught me a little unprepared and I was still the worst for wear. Those guys at the bar hadn't kicked me out until 5 a.m. and I hadn't hydrated much this morning. There were no refreshments on board either. I drifted back into a lovely eye rolling sleep of regretful memory that warped into all kinds of demons with every bump in the dusty Turkish road. And I understood everything beneath my eyelids. We stopped for petrol. I got off the bus, rubbing my head and scratching my eyes. Olivia was in a surprisingly good mood and affectionate towards me, even though I was grumpy and sore headed. I reasoned it was the adventure of going new places. Luckily the service station sold beer.

We set off again and I stayed awake as Taki gave us all history lessons from the front of the bus. There were stories of conflict and hard won independence, historical recounts of heroism and sacrifice from the country that he loved. It turns out that he didn't like the British much. I kept my mouth shut but it was interesting. I wondered what Olivia thought about it but she was busy asking about silk rugs to an Italian family behind us. After my third can of beer I called Taki over to talk about rebellion. He went to school in England for a few years but he despised the country. I kind of agreed with him, but I said that I couldn't see how one empire was better than another, or how you could blame a whole country. I asked him how far back one should hold a grievance? He went back to his post at the front of the bus and avoided eye contact with me. Olivia asked me what I had done now.

Our big stop was Ephesus. We drove through the Necropolis. They buried the dead outside the city walls in those days because of the smell, or the fear. They say there are more people alive now in the world than have ever died. I cannot figure that out. Or did I make that up?

Ephesus is what was. A thriving place not even that long ago, in the history of things, but long enough to be abandoned and to be seen crumbling now. I felt like I was on the set of Jason and the Argonauts. Unreal ruins. Taki gave us some interesting facts about how the place had been a major city, in a strategic position, that had been invaded, taken and used by all the classical empires. He gave me a dirty look. I guess he could hold a grudge forever, and ever. I had never been to Egypt, Athens, Rome, nor Persia. I had been to Stonehenge, but that was tiny and basic, and only impressive in its longevity. Ephesus fascinated me in that I could sense a once thriving place, with people not too dissimilar to myself walking down it's roughly made streets, shopping and whatnot. I could feel a connection to those that were gone now, and I could half imagine their lives. I am simple in that way. I held Olivia's hand as we walked. The world turned.

We got back on the bus and visited a silk rug factory, it was part of the deal, we were tied in. We witnessed the breeding of silk worms and the farming of them to make these human hand-made, beautiful floor coverings, but we couldn't afford to get one. Olivia's taste didn't even border on Turkish anyway. She was into IKEA. I am not one for aggressive salesmen either, or how aggrieved they feel after so many refusals to buy. "No, thanks." I say it to beggars and merchants and prostitutes and street corner pamphleteers without blinking. I find it easy to say no as I have two hundred pounds to my name until next week.

Then we ate somewhere. Hard boiled eggs and meat and olives, all laid out and waiting. There was salad too and water. I ventured into the bar and got a beer. The rest of the bus company had dispersed and were sat on benches drinking Turkish tea when I came out. The bus headed us back to our hotels.

We get back and go out to our regular spot. The Donny lot are there and we end up staying too late again with the raki. Back at the pool we sit around and talk and smoke and try to outdo each other with shit jokes. Olivia is flat out on her stomach and snoring when I flop in to bed.

In the morning I find out that Olivia has booked us on another trip. This time we get to take a boat. It'll be a day

30

jaunt to nearby beauty spots on a big wooden gullet bullet. I am still drunk as she urges me up. No time for coffee. A taxi takes us down to the boat and we board with a bunch of others. My eyes aren't working yet, but it's a big boat. There must be fifty of us passengers. I have sunglasses. We are a little crammed in. Soon we have the excuse of staring in awe at the beauty around us. It's enough to leave anyone speechless, never mind the overhung. Olivia gasps and prods at the scenery and I am responsive but I can tell she is still eyeing the Italian lad in the corner with his shirt off. He is with someone.

The rocks out around the bay and the colour of the sky reflected in the sea, then out there, the blue, it makes all of us feel beautiful. The skip anchors and we see a swimming opportunity. There are other boats and there are whoops of delight as brave ones dive off. We drop off the boat and marvel in the warmth and tranquility of the sea. Then over at the cliffs, there is a splash as someone dives.

Wow!

And as we look up, there are willing divers on top of an outcrop, and as we follow with our eyes the trail of swimmers to the base of the cliff and a trail up to the top. It looks high to me. Olivia, she is a strong swimmer, freestyles off towards the jumping point. I struggle to keep up, breaststroking, and am a little tired as I clamber out after her. She urges me on after her up the rocky path to where the locals are congregating. Some men are walking back down past us gingerly, saying "no way!" When we get up there, with one or two others from our boat, although not the Italian lad, we realise that a lot of them up there are just watching. Sure, they have their swimming gear on but they aren't brave enough to leap. The trail of jumpers and divers are steadily swimming from boats. Oh my. Olivia has no such qualms. Come on, she urges, and takes her step and leaps feet first over the rocks into a god knows what plunge. I see her bikini bum narrowly miss a scrape before she disappears. I daren't look over though. The group of young, local lads gasp and cheer. I don't know what to do, but I know I can't walk back down. I take five steps back and then surge forward. I try to keep my body straight. It takes a while. I am falling. Where is the water? I look down to see where it is. It hits me in the face. I sink. I don't think I even try to get back to the surface, it just happens. Then there is air.

"Are you alright?" Olivia asks. She is laughing. It's funny. It must have looked funny because she can't stop laughing. One of my eyeballs has been pushed backwards into my skull.

"Yes," I say, "I feel sick."

There are a couple of previous jumpers still there in the little pool. "We saw you, that was bad! Are you okay?"

It was the worst entry… I gasp a bit and I find it difficult to swim, or even tread water. Olivia swims ahead, she's still chuckling. When I manage to clamber back onto the boat the captain tells me that they don't recommend that we do that jumping thing that the locals do.

I collapse onto my bag.

I AM IN A DIFFERENT ROOM

I am in a different room
When I hear that female gasp
The panting
My eyes pop open
As if they can listen
They hear that man's voice then
A low register
It's not saying anything
I want to hear
There is a loud smack
And I close my eyes again
And shiver
With fear in my bones

I am in a different room
When I hear that female panting
The gasps
My eyes pop open
To listen in
They hear that man's low moan
It registers
That she is with
My friend right now
And I shut my eyes
Again
With release in my bones

I am in a different room
When I hear a
Gasping
Panting
Female
My eyes pop open
As I realize
My wife is on the exercise bike
And it's time I made the coffee
And I close my eyes
Again
But I have to get up
With pleasure
In my bones

TUTH

Then there was Julie
Livid in a dorm at Sheffield University
Studying anatomical illustration
Where she confessed that she loved to dissect testicles
In the union and the Rugby World Cup was ongoing
Some England lads got a hold there
Partisan in those days
She had a green shirt on
They grabbed her scruff and called her Paddy
I think that's what it was
Idiot maybe? No, thick, Irish twat
That's it
She'd heard it before
She'd been called worse
And she was half
They took it to the corner flag
She rocked back and then launched a ferocious head
Towards the snooty laughter of the one before her
Popping capillaries
His blood spotted the concrete
Red as the angry swine
That then ran after
As she abandoned all thoughts of love to escape
She broke her finger in the crack of a brick wall
Towards her England
Thine
Help
They chased all night

She hid in trees
And then when she thought she heard friends
She appeared in front of 'Them'
Oops!
She offered herself
Just get it over with
And they obliged
Her tooth flying
To lazy
Grateful
Fairies

WE ARE NUNS

I am on a boat full of them, novices anyway, is what they tell me. Out of habit. Me too, is what I am thinking, I haven't had sex for over a month! Or under one. I can't remember or determine. I am drunk… but I was making *polite* chat when I had asked what they all did for a living…

The novices had been noisy and full of themselves, and I was a party to it by proximity on this Dublin ferry floor. They shut me down with that nun shocker so I contented myself with a can of beer. One of them wanted a quieter word though. She waited for the attention to tangent itself before she isolated me.

"What's the matter?" she asked.

"Not much." I lift up the urn and show her. "Ash! No matter really, just my dad."

She knows, by her eyes, that I am cut in half.

"He needs an introduction." I say, as I pat the urn, to make her feel more included. Did I say we were sat on the floor because the ferry was so busy that all the seats had been given up to the infirm? It was choppy outside also.

"I'm Fiona, pleased to meet you." She says, shaking the urn like a hand.

"This is Joe." I put him to my ear, "He likes your freckles."

There's a silence. I guess that was a bit weird.

"You going to drink all of those?" She pointed out the case of Stella Artois I had purchased from the duty free.

"Not possible. Would you like one?"

"Mm!"

I offer what I am cradling to her friends then. "You?"

Her girlfriends decide I'm not worth the bother. They see no potential in me.

"Don't you think you've had enough?" Fiona says.

"Not yet."

"We've just come from a concert, in London." She shrugs.

"How was that?"

"We won." It makes me laugh and look at them all again. I see a unity, a sureness, they're a big-toothed grin of a team.

"Well done." I drink.

"We're celebrating."

"Doesn't look like it." I say.

"You don't have to get... listen.... Come with me."

So I went with her. I had to take my dad.

We went up the carpeted stair onto the top deck. She held the urn whilst I pulled at the wind-stuck, leaden door. We looked out for a while. Then, there, in the howl, and staring at the wake in the dark, she kissed me. I don't know why. I will never know.

"Where are you going?" Fiona asked me, even as I stood there this close to her.

"I'm taking him back."

"Home."

"Yes."

I put the urn down so that I could free my hands. She kissed me more. It was a big snog. I grabbed her arse and she stroked my oysters. She had me.

We promised each other more sunrises. We watched for land. She was beautiful in the glow. And then I started thinking. It was my first time away from Lancashire in ten years. I suddenly felt like a tourist. I wasn't meant to be. I broke away from her and we just stood there, watching our wake. It was awkward. She made herself busy after a while. She smoothed herself down.

"It was nice meeting you."
"It was nice meeting you."

She went back and found her coven. We docked. I gave everyone some space, I watched them disembark, talking, laughing. I think I was the last on deck... Then it hit me. They weren't nuns! They had probably drunk my beer. Dad rolled about the ship in his new and compact plastic house, laughing his arse off.

YACK YACK BACKYARD

The rain stopped on Sunday afternoon, after seven days. Our garden doesn't get swamped for too long as we live half way on a steep hill - the water won't just stand about waiting to evaporate, our basement suffers. We had a sump pump put in so there is no more flooding, our personal deluge ends up in the Hudson. Just like it used to, I guess, before the white man created obstacles.

So the soggy passerines came out in force on Sunday afternoon. They have been waiting to build nests.

In our apple tree I have hung a thistle seed feeder. Some goldfinches own this tree. They will submit, temporarily, to a sparrow, but the charm soon wins over. I wonder where they all live. The ubiquitous sparrows, or most of them, share our eaves and gutters. I recognize one or two of them sometimes. One had a piece of nylon ribbon attached to a foot for a few days. She looked like a small, fluffy balloon escaped from a kid's party.

The peach tree at the back has a more accessible sunflower seed feeder. It's not as niche. Last year I managed to get within whispering distance of a skinny house finch and noticed its eyes were almost glued shut. I also wondered about its' hearing capacity. I read that there could be some kind of salmonella affecting the bird - food poisoning. It could be my fault. I started to wash the feeders regularly after that, although I didn't notice any other birds that were afflicted. What puzzled me was how it found the feeder. Do finches have a keen sense of smell?

A plague of grackles came by one day. They perched high in our neighbour's shaggy pine and then invaded, pushing out all except a merl of red-winged blackbirds, themselves the wispy end of a cloudy migration.

In the dogwood to the side of the house I hung two feeders, one is squirrel proof (as much as anything can be) but the other isn't. I don't mind them all sharing and I actually scatter critter food about in winter like Brenda Fricker in Home Alone 2. We have two red tailed squirrels, a black squirrel, and maybe three or more of the all grey squirrels. They come and go, family. They live over the road in another neighbour's house. He sets traps for them so that they aren't running around his attic. Friendly traps. Then he drives them 50 miles away and releases them upstate. And here I am feeding them and wondering if they miss each other.

The radiant cardinals, I have noticed, pair off and are extremely territorial. I hardly ever see more than two at a time, unless they are fighting. Do they deserve a collective noun? It's the same with wrens, they are aggressively antisocial to their own kind. Some males will fight over a female even if she is already incubating her eggs. A successful interloper will get rid of the eggs of his defeated predecessor and start again. We have a nesting box in front and one male wren has been putting himself about there, singing his syrinx out whilst still building. For what? I feel for him, but he could be the other guy. I've herd of wrens (a sic pun) but this is ridiculous.

The songs of the wren and the cardinal are nothing compared to the mockingbird and starling, but I do find them easier to identify. Mockingbirds, I only ever see solitary, I hear their echoes though, similar to the mewing catbird, and I could listen to them all day.

The starlings here, in our backyard, aren't great in number, so we don't see those beautiful swooping murmurations at dusk as we did in Brighton in the UK. I don't know what goes on there. Maybe they have some collective consciousness, a hive mind. I know that starlings were introduced here in NY, in 1910's or close to that, and maybe they have swollen in number nationally, but in certain places there are not enough of them to put on those displays. Why do they do it anyway, just because they can, like gulls boomeranging in the wind? Are they so happy to see each other after a hard day? Why don't they all just settle down and sleep? Or is it because when there is such a massive, chattering number of them they attract raptors that then try and take advantage of some late supper. Is the beautiful starling sky ballet just mass hysteria?

I had never seen a nuthatch until I moved into this house, now at least one is a regular visitor, as are the woodpeckers, there are at least four of those, but not together, never together. The nuthatch can share time at the feeder with the chickadees but every one is out of there when the sparrows come around. The sparrows fill their bellies, whereas the nuthatches and woodpeckers, and the chickadees, will take some and store it and come back. It depends on the time of day also, and what they want to eat. I don't think the woodpeckers are interested in coming down so far to our yard when the earth warms and grubs become available.

The mourning doves content themselves with the spilled husks. Now sometimes there are a few of those birds, skulking about the grass, heads bowed. There could be six or eight of them. So I would say they could deserve a collective noun like, a 'funereal procession of mourning doves'. Slightly long winded, I know, but no more ridiculous than 'a parliament of owls'. I've seen a few owls, but they were always by themselves. Some birds just do not need a collective term.

A splattering of robins?

A dash of osprey?

Talking of which…

From above, our houses, our gardens, our yards, this land is not separate. The boiling hawks, the kettling vultures see only the traps we have put out and the bait eating the traps.

Last winter I saw a red-tailed hawk perched on our snow-laden privet hedge, the flakes were big and soft that day and still falling. Maybe the bird's feathers were wet and it was tired from a meatless hunt. As I tried to capture a photograph, the hawk flew up into whiteness. I should have taken out a steak from the fridge for it. A different hawk on a different day had figured it out though and was feasting on a sparrow in the snow by our shed. I got closer to this one but it took hold of what it was tearing into and flew just over my woolly head as I fluffed towards it. I couldn't tell what it was. My first thought was sparrowhawk, but things are different here in the USA, in NY, in Yonkers, in the snow.

NEITHER ONE THING NOR T'OTHER

"You know?"
My dad said
About to spout
Ready to expel
Usually it was gas
But sometimes
Every now and then
An insightful bubble
Came out with the rubbish
Old fashioned wisdom
With its reek
What he said was
"There are two kinds of people in this world
And you're not one of them."

TURKEY EGGS

Within the dark
There is a darker place
An impatient lump batters the bone
A little man kicks at the cracks
It's a strange room
An oubliette
And locked in
Thoughtlessness
Dumb reactions from this fist
These feet
This knee jerk

Where is the light
Where are the ideas
What is on the blister on the tip of my tongue
What is for breakfast
Why don't we eat turkey eggs

I know
All it takes is the question
These things are in place for traditional reason
It only takes a phone call to the swan police
For you to stop asking
Chickens don't give a flying feck for their brood
But turkey's do
Tuck that neck in
Salt your small omelette
Shut up

MUSTARD MITT

The sky is blue today
It isn't always
But it's up there
Like my dog's eyebrows

I ask her for some answers but
She just looks confused

Dogs!

That's what I say
Out loud
Whilst she squats
And urinates on our patch of earth
Before padding off to her safe zone
To think unimaginable thoughts
I think on her trickle
Infiltrating the minerals
Stood here on the porch remembering mine then
Like I just planted asparagus
Of course
Under a blue sky
And a red moon
Paws of clay
That I will have to towel down now
Or face the wrath of my wife

In!
I say
In!
Let's escape

SKEETERS

Why aren't they back yet
Because I told them to quiet
As the cold
Between us
I fear
How rampant they will be this year
With that animal thrust
The most lusty must have
And a thirst for blood
Just in the eyes of these young
Only feeling things
Knowing all of life

REAL WINDOW

There's some kerfuffle down on the river
Not even a binocular can determine
It's stopped flowing in the middle
A dead pool
And white birds swarm
From here anyway
In a silent frenzy

A couple of hours later
I wait as the carcass
Washes in

On the slow ebb of the land licking river

It's only a duck
Fresh kill
Pecked clean
Eaten out by gulls
That had seen off a heron
And a pelican
With yellow eyes
And mad screams

BOWERY DIME MUSEUM

I've seen a bearded baby here
That never made the news
Unlike the fearless lady
With her daily tattooed shoes
I heard tell there was a politician
Who smiled without a tooth
She was just invented yesterday
So appeals to this year's youth
There are newborns every minute here
There are punters by the score
Mods obsessed with yesteryear
Are always back for more
Lots of freakish normalcy down at The Bowery Dime
    Museum
All expositions for a dollar you should come and see 'em
There are eunuchs' sons from antiquity
In virgins' daughters laps
And two faced tv presenting monkeys
Who offer each other claps
Lots of modern freakery down at The Bowery Dime Museum
If you perchance can spare a dollar then you'll get to see 'em
Roll up here for the bombardier, armless in his trousers
See the Kaiser's wax moustache tackled by some Scousers
Underneath the trestle are mice as big as cats
And once inside the armoire they procreate with rats
There are cage free Wall Street tigers
Exclaiming carpe diem
But you'll be safe

They've got the dope down at the Bowery Dime Museum
There's an elephant painting tables
And a pig that waits your easel
There's a stoat in a coat
Created by Zeus
And a naked lady weasel
Lots of yadda yadda
Down at the dumdy dum
You should pickle herring
It's possibly more fun
There's salad that's eating models
There's fags that are smoking butts
There's sex starved Sheeney on his hole machine
Siphoning his nuts
Lots of smoke and mirrors
Down at The Bowery Dime Museum
You're not worth the price of entry if you can't even see 'em

MOFONGO

It's the first day we've been able to lie out. The atmosphere has been moody. Here we are though on the loungers. And the surf mashes onto the buttery sand behind us. We have brought a book each but are soon distracted by an iguana. It wanders into vision about twenty feet away on the grass fringed with coconut palms. The lizard is big and its tail tapers off to a seemingly infinite point. It is unafraid and its movements are elegant. Then it stops. A smaller one, more colourful, scampers up alongside. This one has a crest and seems a little skittish... *Are you watching?* Yes, I say. Everyone is.

The small one climbs on to the scaly spine of the first. They stay like that for ten minutes. Maybe more. I look at my book but can't finish a sentence. Some kids from the chalet next door come and take photographs. It looks like a mother giving its baby a ride, as chimps cling to the breast, but I guess they are just having sex.

They are not having sex!

I sip a little rum as he gets his spuds in slowly. Is it the way of it here in the tropics? They don't seem to care there by the bar, a stone skip from the sea, as the waves break and break again...

THE MULTICULTURAL SQUIRRELS OF TOMPKINS SQUARE SHAPED PARK

A crew of dark eyed juncoes
Quarrel in the trees
With ubiquitous old world sparrows
And a banditry of chickadees
Call to their sweeties
Under a boil of hawks
Yet the squirrels do not care
For the air
Beneath their feet
They get on with anyone until dusk

SONGS IN HONKY BARS

Stop for a second
And then maybe a third
How it might be golden here
But guilt edged
Should you even pause
Taking your sweet time out
Away from that bitter half at home
The same football game is on the screen
Just across the street
That bar full of seer suckered successful men drinking
    whiskey
Throbs to funk as they dance and discuss the bill
And closing out Vanessa
Because we have two tabs here
Vanessa!
And one is for the appetizers
And one is for the drinks
And what is the difference
Is it just a lack of subtlety
We nod and shuffle to Sigur Ros
You can't understand
The sacrifice of rhythm
For the tonk tonk tonk
But this here is drinking music
There is always tangible excitement
Imbibers' voices drowning in beer drowning the sounds
Pale Ale takes over the PA
This white collar cellar bar

How it pretends to dive
Like an aerated whale
Sometime you will stop being an observer
And partake
But here is comfort
Of a similar class
Because you will not be asked
Anything
Unless you drain your glass

IBIZAN RAPTURES

We can sit and look
At the excavated serra
Under this blisterful sun
Halfway on a dry pined terrace
Whilst the cicadas engines overrun
We will be bitten
By tiny predators
And again
Submerge stinging skin
One evening in the middle of July
Before a moon falls
Ants appear
Hundreds fly and die
Dimpling the surface of the warm pool
We cannot swim for fear of mouthfuls
Hundreds more lose their queen
And divested of wings
Busy themselves amongst crumbs
Under the alfresco table
Where the lizards roam
On a feast day
They dally in the glow
Not scared by feet for once
But reaping slowly with silent tongues

MANUAL FOR POSTMEN

None of this is difficult
You take your van and fill it
Later you empty the items
One by one
Until they are all gone
If you don't deliver
You will be let go
Like a boxed out fighter
Or a bettered lover

A VALERIE LYRIC

My life was simple
And single
Until you created a turmoil
I wish for so much from this
But will settle for a kiss to calm me
Settle for some of that
Breath back
You took
Last time we met

SMITH'S ONION

The kids burst out of the aquarium and run, whoop whoop! onto the sand. They perform cartwheels and flips as their teachers order hot dogs for the lot of them. An old lady does her tai chi a little further down the beach, watched or ignored by the big, black-backed gulls on the rock. I can taste salt in the air. I shouldn't really be here.

When you're off work sick you should have the decency to stay in bed, and not behave like a tourist.

I got to thinking about Smithson, having recently visited one of his many museums. I had discovered that he conducted experiments detailing the chemical content of a lady's teardrop. I wondered why hers would be any different than mine, but I guess they just are.

Printed in the United States
By Bookmasters